The Lyre Handbook:

Playing Methods of the Anglo-Saxon Lyre With Directions for Construction

By Mary K. Savelli

© 2011 Mary K. Savelli
All Rights reserved.

Table of Contents

Introduction 4
Construction 5
Playing Techniques 7
Playing Chords 17
    C and Dm 17
    F and G7 18
    Am and G 20
    Additional Chords 20
Bibliography 22

Introduction

The Anglo-Saxon lyre was the instrument commonly used by the *scop*, or Anglo-Saxon poet. The lyre belongs to the psaltery family of instruments, which also includes the bowed psaltery, the hammer dulcimer, the harp and the zither. The term *psalter* comes from the Greek *psallo*, meaning "to twang". The Old English verb, *hearpian*, has a similar meaning, "to harp" or "to play upon, pluck." *Hearpe* is the noun form of *hearpian*, which was used for both harps and lyres, meaning "that which is plucked".

It is uncertain when the first Germanic lyres were made. Archeological finds date back as early as the sixth century. There have been half a dozen grave finds, and nearly a dozen bridges found, the most famous of which are the pieces recovered from the Sutton Hoo royal burial. From these finds and from illuminations such as those in the Vespasian *Psalter* and the Durham *Cassiodorus*, historians have been able to reconstruct the instrument. The lyre is a wooden stringed instrument, rounded on both ends, between 20" and 30" in length. It was usually made of oak or maple with a bridge of amber, bone or wood. The lower half of the body was hollow, forming the sound box. The top was opened in an oval. The only evidence for sound holes comes from the Trossinger lyre, which has tiny holes drilled above and below the bridge. The strings, which are believed to have been of gut, numbered from four to eight, but there were usually six. (See Figure 1.)[1]

In his *De harmonica institutione*, a Frisian monk named Hucbald uses the *hexachord* when describing the notes of the lyre. A hexachord is a six-note pattern used to teach sight singing and usually began on C, continuing with D, E, F, G, and A. This tuning is supported by carvings on the Trossinger lyre. While I use the hexachord throughout this book, please feel free to experiment with different tunings.

Manuscript illuminations demonstrate that the lyre was played both with the fingers and the plectrum, (from *plektron*, "thing to strike with"). A famous example is the portrait of David from the Vespasian *Psalter*, showing the player muting the strings with the left hand while strumming with the right. The Estonian kannel, an instrument evolved from the Germanic lyre, is played by strumming with muted strings to accompany singing, but plucked when playing fast dance tunes. While the exact method used by the Anglo-Saxons is still debated, the lyre may have been strummed for accompanying poetry and plucked for playing instrumental music. Both of these methods are taught in this booklet.

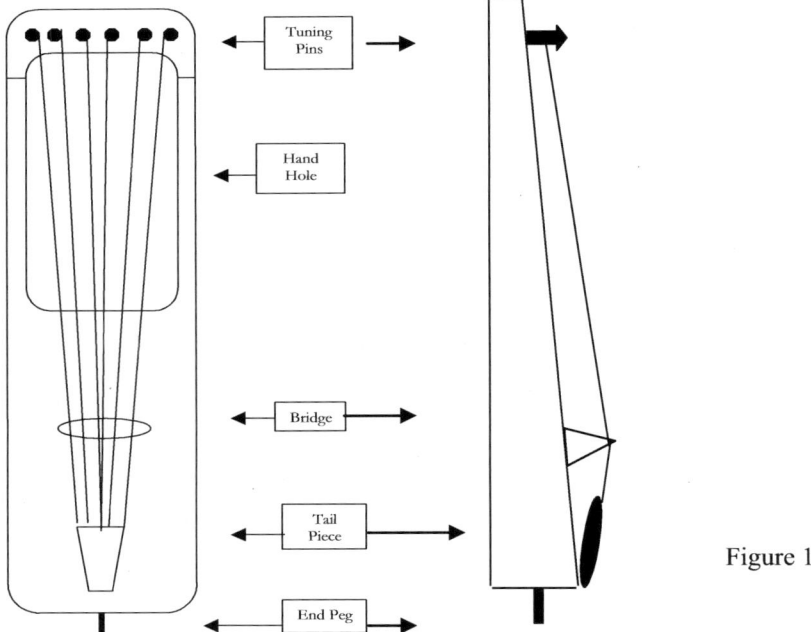

Figure 1.

---

[1] Continental evidence also suggests that the back of the lyre was angled. The construction plans in this booklet are for the more common flat back. If you are a skilled woodworker, however, you can angle the back making the depth 1¼" at the bottom and ¾" at the top.

Construction

This method of construction calls for three pieces of wood: a back piece, a thin sounding board, and a reinforcing piece for the tuning peg area.[2] Figure 3 shows an outline drawing of the lyre, giving the dimensions for this design.[3] For the back, you need one 8" x 30" piece of a hard wood, preferably oak or maple. It should be ¾" to 1¼" thick. For the sounding board, or belly, you will need a 8" x 30" piece of ⅛" thick hardwood or hardwood laminate (plywood). For the top or reinforcing piece, you will need a section approximately ¼" x 3" x 8", with the grain running cross-wise in relation to the body. (This can be cut from the same board as the back or body, since you will likely have to purchase a piece longer than the 30" needed.)

You will also need 6 tuning pins, 6 strings, a tail-piece and a bridge. If you are unable to carve or find lyre pins, you can use harp or violin pins. Brass brads are optional. Read through all the directions before starting.

Step 1. CUT OUT BACK PIECE.
   a) Make a pattern based on Figures 2 and 3. Be sure to include the internal markings, such as the curve at the bottom center. (This is to allow enough solid area when you drill the end peg hole.)
   b) Trace the pattern onto the 8" x 30". Cut external dimensions. Cut out the hand hole. Mark the hole for the end peg.

Step 2. ROUTE OUT SOUND BOX.
   a) Route out the sound box to a depth where ⅛" of the wood remains.
   b) Cut away a ¼" deep section from the top of body to allow the cross-grain piece to fit.
   c) Check the pattern to the back. If it no longer fits, create a new pattern for belly. (You do not need to mark the sound box.)

Step 3. CUT OUT BELLY.
   a) Trace pattern on remaining pieces. Cut out the belly and the cross-grain piece, leaving the hand hole intact.
   b) Glue belly and top piece in place. Clamp and allow to dry.
   c) Turn lyre with belly face down. Cut out hand hole following the opening in the back piece.

Step 4. FINISHING THE INSTRUMENT.
   a) Mark and drill the tuning-pin holes about 1" apart. (If you are using tapered pins, buy the reamer and tuning key from the same supplier to ensure a proper fit.)
   b) Drill the hole for the end peg.
   c) Sand and finish the wood with linseed oil or a commercial sealant.
   d) Insert the tuning pins and the end peg. (You can use a violin end peg or make your own from a piece of dowel rod.)
   [e) If you wish, you can nail down the top with small brass brads, spaced ⅛" from the edges, approximately 2" apart.]

Step 5. STRINGING THE LYRE.
   a) Choose your strings. I recommend nylon guitar strings. If you can purchase them separately, use three (3) B, or 2nd, strings and three (3) G, or 3rd, strings. If you can only find sets, buy two sets and use the G, B and E, or 1st, strings.
   b) Attach the strings to the tail piece, starting with the lowest (thickest) string on the right side of the lyre. If your strings have balls on the ends, simply slide them through the holes on the tail piece. If not, you will need to tie them with a square knot.
   c) Attach the tail-piece to the end peg. You can use gut, sinew or cotton embroidery floss. If using either of the latter two, you will need to thread it through the end-strap holes several times before you tie it off. (If you cannot find a suitable tail piece and raised bridge, you can make your own using the patterns in Figure 4, located inside the back cover. Note that the end-strap holes in the tailpiece are drilled at a slight angle.)
   d) Attach the strings to the tuning pins, starting with the outside two and working toward the center. Only turn them to take up the slack. When all of the strings are attached, place the bridge under the strings and with a pencil, mark where the strings rub. Remove the bridge, score the marks with a file and replace it. Then, tune the lyre to Middle C, D, E, F, G and A. (You may want to tune them slightly flat. Let the strings stretch over-night and finish tuning the next

---

[2] This method is based on Option 2 in Priest-Dorman.

[3] These dimensions are based on the Sutton Hoo reconstruction.

day.) The lyre may need to be re-tuned every day for some time.

If you want, you can tie a leather stap around the two sides of the hand hole. When playing the lyre, you can slip your hand through the strap and it will help you support the lyre in an upright position.

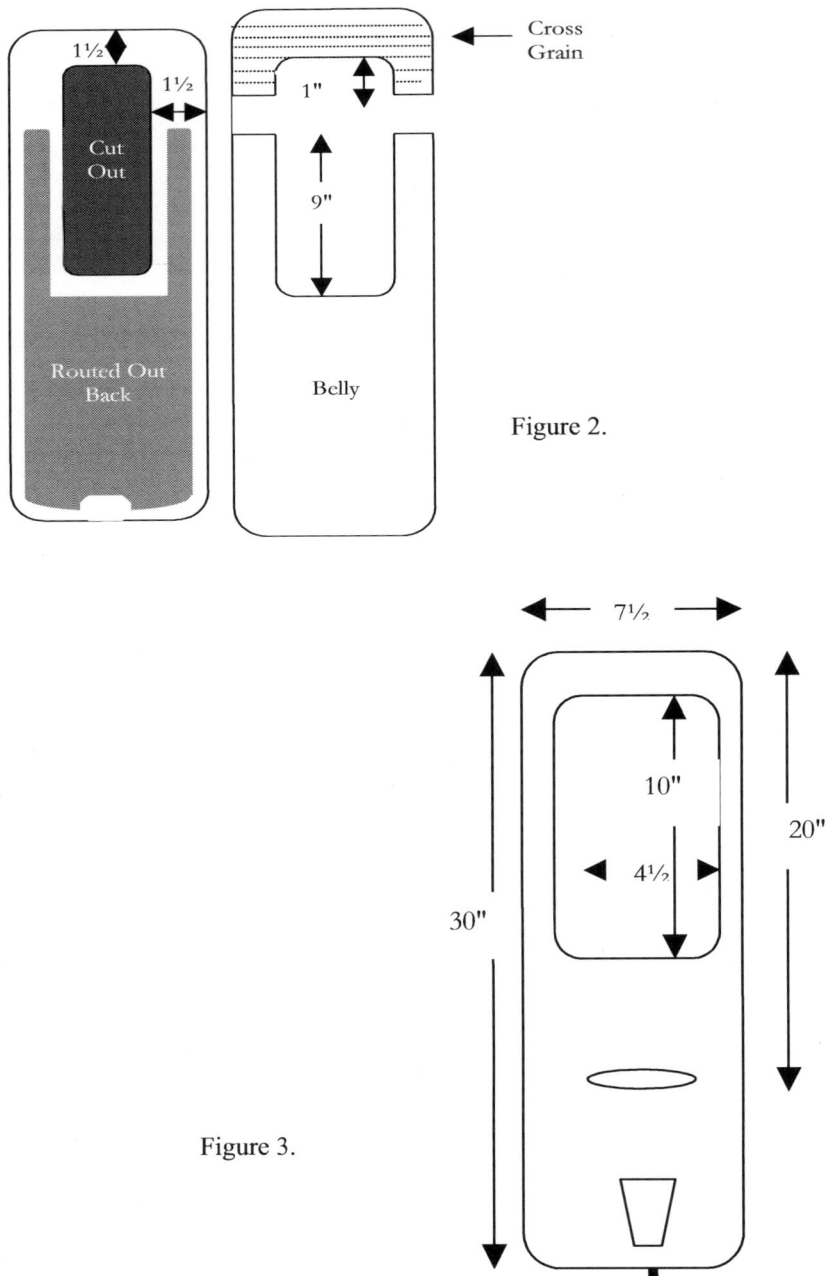

Figure 2.

Figure 3.

Playing Techniques

To start, we will review some musical terms and notation. If you cannot read music, you may find it helpful to buy a basic book on the subject.

<u>Staff</u>: The five lines (and four spaces) onto which notes are placed.
<u>Clef</u>: The symbol at the beginning of the staff, which indicates the pitches of the lines and spaces.
<u>Bar Lines</u>: Vertical lines which mark off the measures, or the units, of the staff.
<u>Time Signature</u>: The numbers at the beginning of a staff. The top number tells how many beats are in a measure. The bottom tells you which type of note receives one (1) count. For example, in 4/4 or common time (C), the measure lasts for four beats and each quarter note receives one beat.
<u>Notes</u>: The circles placed on the staff. The notation system is based on the whole note (a circle with no stem). Each note is slightly different, marking a fraction of a whole note. For example, a half note, which differs by adding a stem, is one-half (½) as long as a whole note. The quarter note, which differs from the half by being filled in, lasts one-fourth (¼) of a whole note.
<u>Pitch</u>: The specific tone of a note. Pitches are named for the first 7 letters of the alphabet. Students easily remember the pitches of the spaces in the Treble clef because they spell "**FACE**". You can remember the names of the lines with the saying, "**E**very **G**ood **B**oy **D**oes **F**ine."

There are two basic techniques used to play the Anglo-Saxon lyre. The first method is to pluck the strings. With this technique, you can play melodies and fingerpick chords. The second method is the mute-and-strum method. With this technique you can strum chords. Both methods use the same playing position. Lean the lyre toward your left shoulder and support it with the palm of your left hand. Try holding the lyre closer or farther from your body, adjusting the angle until you find a position which is comfortable.

We will begin with the picking technique. To play a note, pick the string by pulling the pad of your finger-tip towards you, catching it on the string. In this section, I suggest which finger to use on which string. These are only suggestions. When you practice try different fingers and use whichever ones work best for you.

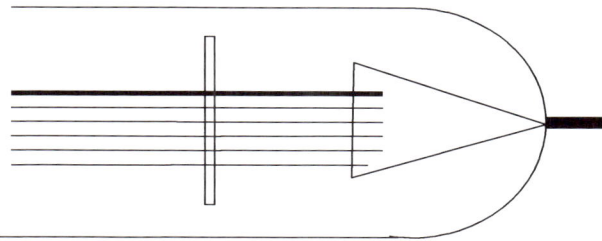

This is **A**.[4] Practice playing the A-string with the index finger, the middle finger and the ring finger.

Whole notes ○ receive 4 beats. Whole rests ▬ receive four counts.

---

[4] The strings are shown parallel for clarity, and do not reflect how they actually appear.

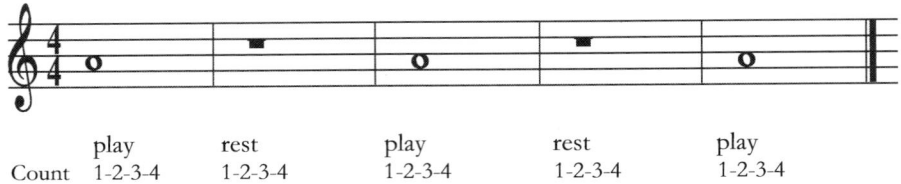

| Count | play
1-2-3-4 | rest
1-2-3-4 | play
1-2-3-4 | rest
1-2-3-4 | play
1-2-3-4 |

Playing A

Count 1-2-3-4

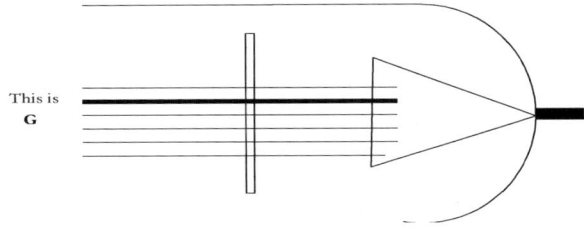

This is G

Practice playing the G-string with the index finger, the middle finger and the ring finger.

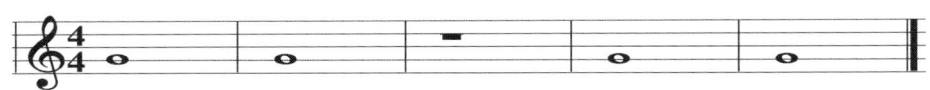

First practice these pieces using the index finger on the G-string and the middle finger on the A-string. Next practice them using the middle finger on the G-string and the ring finger on the A-string.

Two Tones

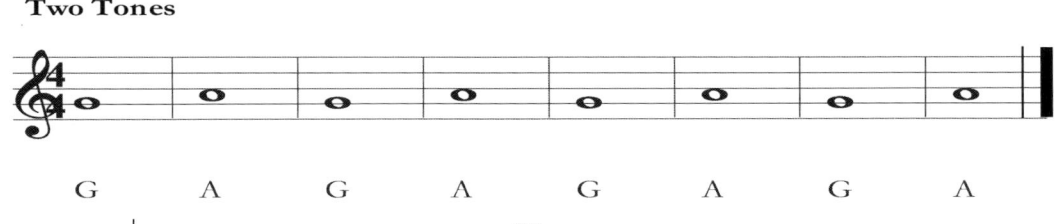

G A G A G A G A

Half-notes ♩ receive 2 counts. The half rest ▬ receives 2 beats.

Back and Forth

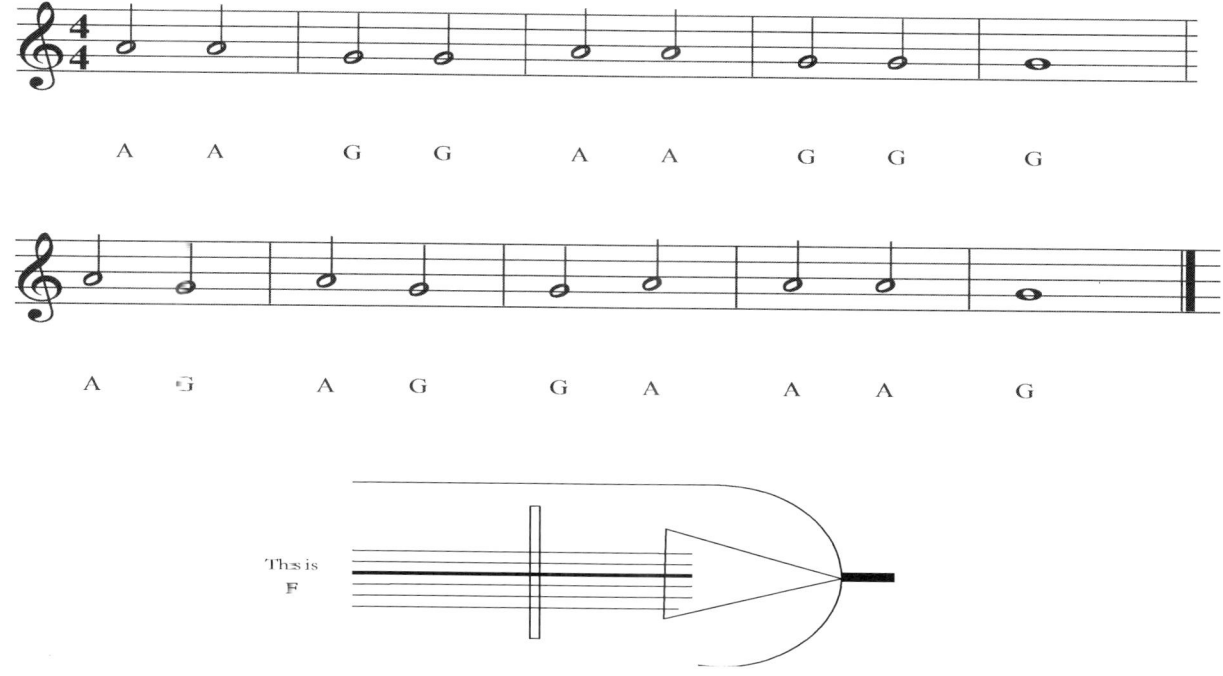

Practice playing the F-string with the index finger, the middle finger and the ring finger.

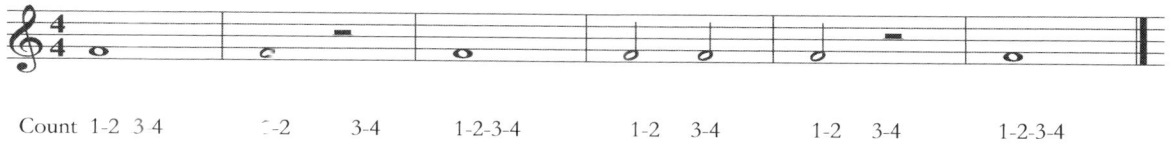

Count 1-2 3-4   1-2   3-4   1-2-3-4   1-2   3-4   1-2   3-4   1-2-3-4

In the following songs, play each string with the finger noted, "i" for the index finger, "m" for the middle finger, and "r" for the ring finger.

G and A meet F

![A repeat sign symbol]

A repeat sign is a double line with two dots. When you reach the "close section" bar, (the double line preceded by the dots) the first time, return to the "open section" bar, (the bar followed by the dots). If there is no "open section" bar, return to the beginning of the song.

The quarter note ♩ receives 1 count; four (4) quarter notes = one (1) whole note.

Four Count

Mary Had A Little Lamb

Special or different endings are shown with numbers. The first time through the song, play to the repeat sign. The second time through, play to the number 1, then skip to the number 2.

Now Spring

In the following piece, play the single notes with your index finger and the double notes with the thumb and middle finger

Bubbles

This is
E.

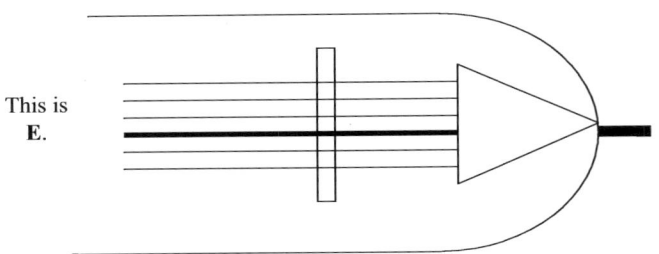

Practice playing the E-string with the thumb, the index finger, and the middle finger.

We will use "t" for "thumb".   The quarter rest receives one (1) beat.

Up We Go

Walking Fingers

Double Bubbles

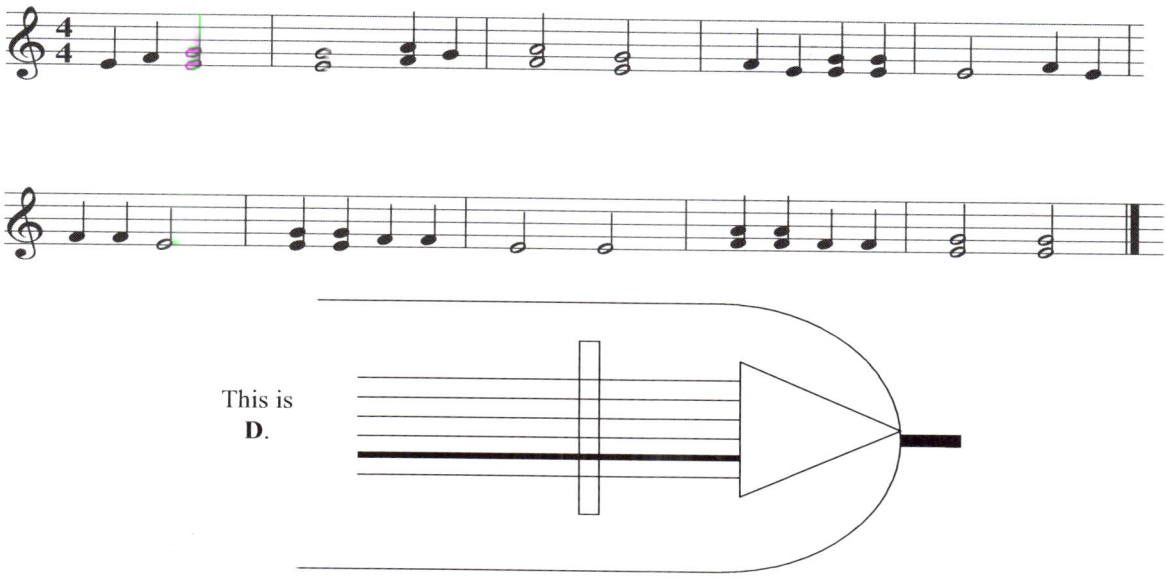

This is **D**.

Practice playing the D-string with the thumb, the index finger, and the middle finger.

Ties ∪ are shown with a curved line connecting two notes. This means you add the beats of the two notes together and play it as if it were one long note.

Playful Five

Dance of Twos

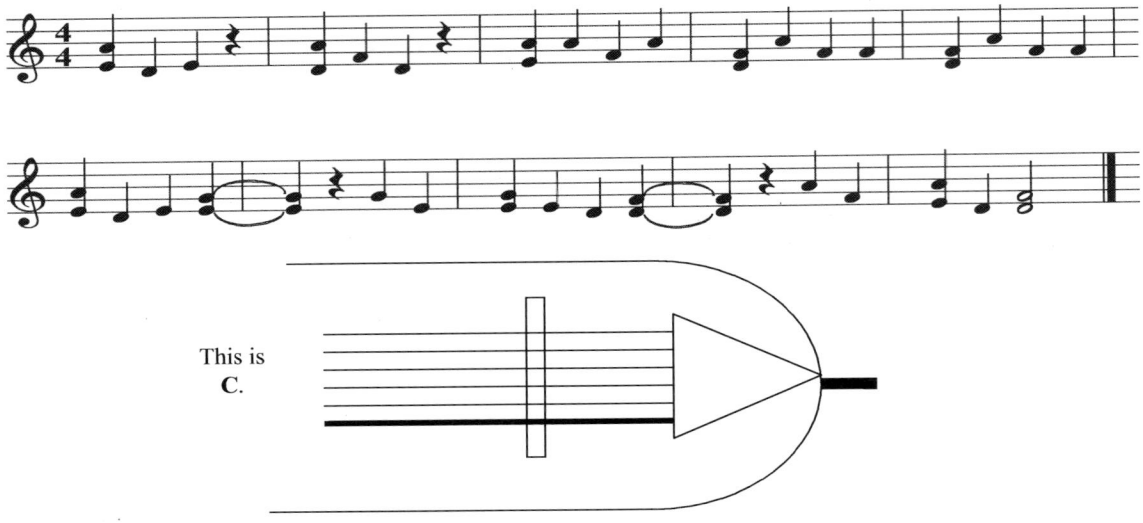

This is C.

Practice playing the C-string with the thumb, the index finger and the middle finger.

Tanzy

A dotted note is counted 1½ times its normal count. For example, a dotted half-note receives three (3) beats.

Liverpool

Dance of Bourgogne

Shall I Come Sweet Love

Thomas Champion

Playing Chords

To play chords while picking, either pluck all three notes at one time, or play each note separately, using the thumb on the lowest note.

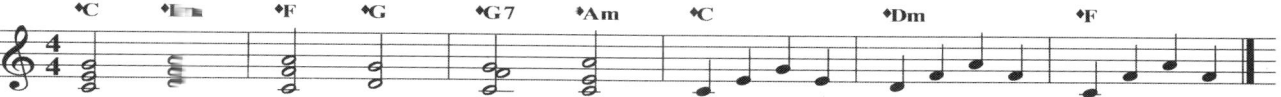

For the mute-and-strum method of play, the left hand's fingers mute the strings that are not used for a particular chord. Touch the strings lightly; do not push up on them. It may take a while to find a position in which you can comfortably support the lyre and mute the strings at the same time. With a pick, you can strum loud enough to cover most of the pluck of the muted strings. This added percussive quality, however, is part of the lyre's unique sound.

Strum in the direction away from your body, holding the pick firmly. At first you should simply practice one strum per beat. Once you become familiar with changing chords, you can strum on the return (as you pull the pick back to the starting position). This will give you two strums per beat. Using this rhythm can vary the harmony.

The following songs use eighth notes ♪ and eighth rests, which each receive one-half (½) of a beat. They also include sixteenth notes which receive one-fourth (¼) of a beat.

Practice these two chords, strumming ↓ ↓ ↓ ↓, counting 1 - 2 - 3 - 4.

---

[5] The circles on the following chord charts show which strings are muted.

I Once Loved a Boy

F chord   G7 Chord

Practice all four chords using the strum pattern ↓ ↓ ↓ ↓↑, counting 1 - 2 - 3 - 4+. The last arrow represents a strum towards you on the second half of the beat.

Am chord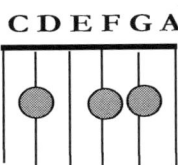

G chord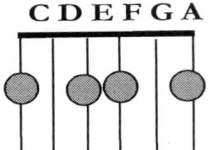

Practice the strum pattern ↓ ↓↑ ↓ ↓↑, counting 1 - 2+ - 3 - 4+.

Additional Chords

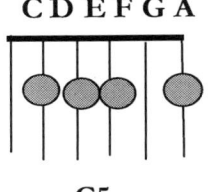

C5

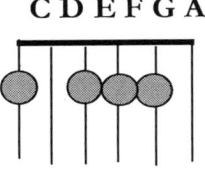

D5

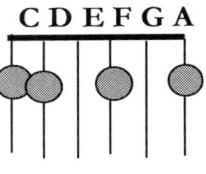

Em

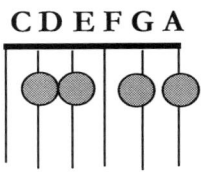

Fm

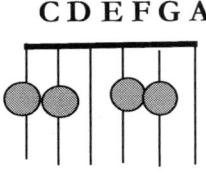

A5

Whiskey in the Jar

Traditional

Bibliography

Bollard, John K. "Playing *Beowulf*: The Sutton Hoo Hearpe and the Performance of Old English Poetry." Paper delivered at The Fortieth International Congress of Medieval Studies, Kalamazoo, MI. 7 May 2005

Bruce-Mitford, Myrtle and Bruce-Mitford, Rupert. "The Sutton Hoo Lyre, 'Beowulf' and the Origins of the Frame Harp," in *Aspects of Anglo-Saxon Archaeology: Sutton Hoo and Other Discoveries.* New York: Harper and Row, 1974, pp. 188-197.

Cable, Thomas. *The Meter and Melody of* Beowulf. Illinois Studies in Language and Literature 64. Urbana: University of Illinois Press, 1974.

Creed, Robert Payson. *Reconstructing the Rhythm of Beowulf.* Columbia: University of Missouri Press, 1990.

Denyer, Ralph, Guillory, Isaac, and Crawford, Alastair M. *The Guitar Handbook.* New York: Alfred A. Knopf, 1982.

Grout, Donald Jay. *A History of Western Music.* Revised ed. New York: W.W. Norton and Co., 1973.

Haas, Ain. *Handbook on Playing Styles for Small Kannels.* Indianapolis: N.p., 1999.

____. *Nationalism and Internationalism in Tracing the Kannel's Origin.* Paper presented at Jalkala Museum Conference, Zelenogorsk, Russia, August 16, 1998.

Hall, J. R. Clark. *A Concise Anglo-Saxon Dictionary.* 4th ed. Cambridge: Cambridge University Press, 1960. Reprinted with a Supplement by Herbert D. Meritt. Toronto: University of Toronto Press for the Medieval Academy of America, 1984. (ISBN 0-8020-6548-1)

Hucbald. "De harmonica institutione" in *Patrologia cursus completus,* series *latina,* edited by J. P. Migne, 221 vols. Paris: Garnier, 1844-1904, 132:905-29. Republished in electronic format in *Thesaurus Musicarum Latinarum.* Bloomington: Indiana University, School of Music, n.d. (http://www.music.indiana.edu/tml/start.html)

Kerman, Frederick Earle. *Trophy Elementary Recorder Method with Baroque and German Fingering.* Cleveland: Trophy Music, 1968.

Kerman, Joseph. *Listen.* 3rd Edition. New York:Worth Publishers, Inc., 1980.

Lueke, Jane-Marie. *Measuring Old English Rhythm: An Application of the Principles of Gregorian Chant Rhythm to the Meter of Beowulf.* Literary Monographs 9. Madison: University of Wisconsin Press, 1978.

Noteworthy Composer™. Fuquay-Varina, NC: Noteworthy Artware, 1998.

Pope, John Collins. *The Rhythm of Beowulf.* New Haven: Yale University Press, 1942.

Priest-Dorman, Greg, and Priest-Dorman, Carolyn. *The Saxon Lyre: History, Construction, and Playing Techniques.* Published in an electronic format. N.p.: N.p., 1995. (http://www.cs.vassar.edu/~priestdo/lyre.html)

The Oxford English Dictionary, 2nd ed., CD-ROM, Oxford: Oxford University Press, 1992.

The Renaissance Guitar. Selected and transcribed by Frederick Noad. New York: Amsco Publications, 1974.

Schueller, Herbert M. *The Idea of Music: An Introduction to Musical Aesthetics in Antiquity and Middle Ages.* Early Drama, Art, and Music Monographs Series, 9. Kalamazoo: Medieval Institute Publications, 1988.

Sherman, Bernard D. *Inside Early Music: Conversations with Performers.* New York: Oxford University Press, 1997.

Solomon, Maynard, ed. *The Joan Baez Songbook.* New York: Ryerson Music Publishers, 1964.

Soodlum's Irish Ballad Book. London: Oak Publications, 1982.

"Tossinger Lyre." Published in an electronic format. N.p.: N.p.,N.d. (https://de.wikipedia.org/wiki/Trossinger_Leier)

Vanin, Claudio. *Musical Form and Tonal Structure in Troubadour Song.* Published in an electronic format. N.p.: N.p., 1994. (http://www.troubadours.vaninedit.com/chapter_V.html)

Wessberg, Erik Axel. *Dromte mig en drom.* CD liner notes. Hojbjerg, Denmark: Tidsskriftet Skalk, 1996. (Translation provided by Ain Haas.)

Thanks to Pat Savelli, Eric Biljum, Sven Lugar, Lary Smith, Ymir Vilmeid and Greg Priest-Dorman for their suggestions and corrections. All remaining errors are my own. And a special thanks goes to Greg for his permission to use contruction directions closely based on his. For more construction details, see his web-site.

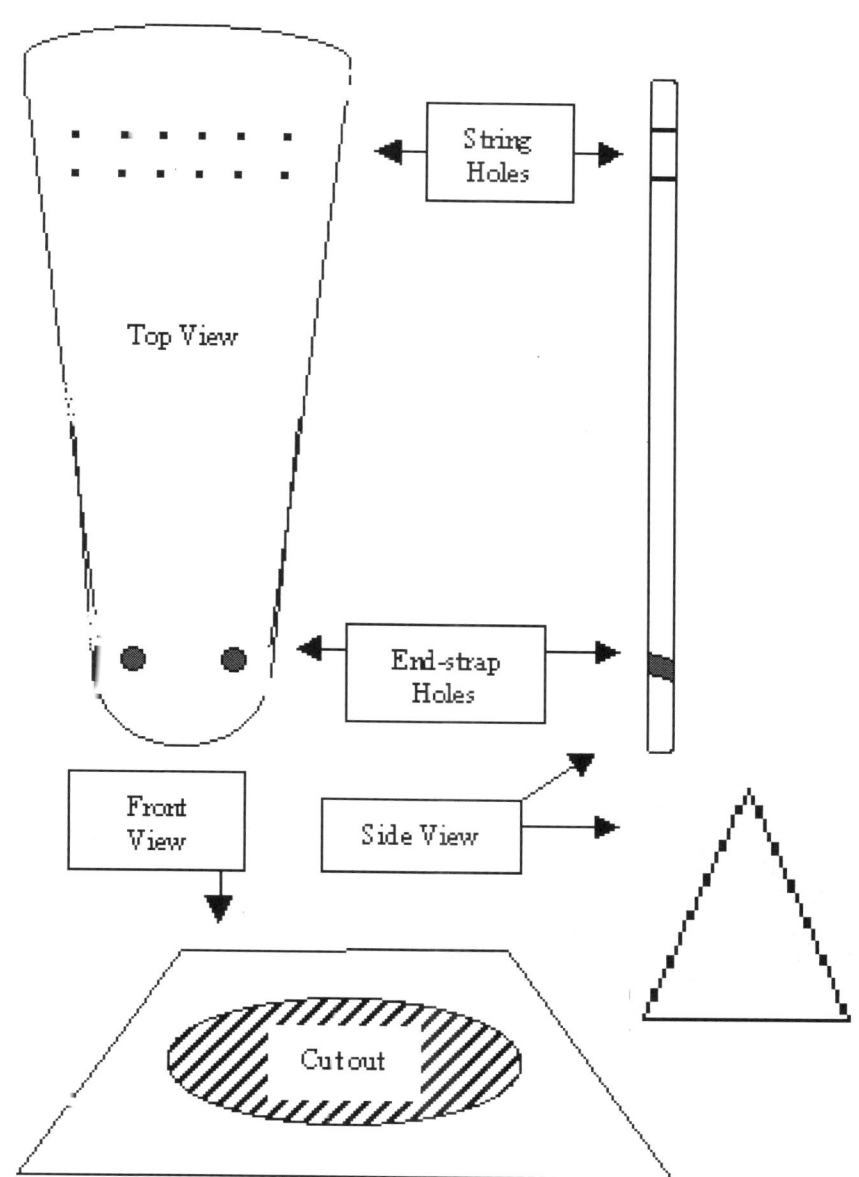

Figure 4. (Actual size)

This page left blank.

Printed in Great Britain
by Amazon